Take-Along Guide

# Planets, Moons and Stars

by Laura Evert
illustrations by Linda Garrow

NORTHWORD PRESS
Chanhassen, Minnesota

## AUTHOR'S NOTE

The planets, moons and stars are constantly changing. As more powerful telescopes are built and probes travel farther into space, scientists make new discoveries. Be sure to check the newspaper for information on events like eclipses and meteor showers that you can see from your home. The most fun way to learn is by looking into the night sky ourselves. The constellations in this book are among the easiest to see in North America. By learning about their history, you learn the history of humankind.

NorthWord Press
18705 Lake Drive East
Chanhassen, MN 55317
1-800-328-3895
www.northwordpress.com

Illustrations by Linda Garrow
Book design by Russell S. Kuepper

**Library of Congress Cataloging-in-Publication Data**
Evert, Laura, 1967-
Planets, moons, and stars / by Laura Evert ;
illustrations by Linda Garrow.
p. cm. – (Take-along guide)
ISBN 1-55971-842-0 (softcover) 1-55971-877-3 (hardcover)
1. Planets—Juvenile literature. 2. Stars—Juvenile literature.
I. Garrow, Linda. II. Title. III. Series.
QB602 .E84 2003
2002032588

Printed in Malaysia
10 9 8 7 6 5 4 3 2 1

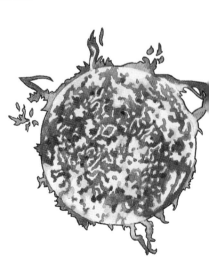

# CONTENTS

Planets, Moons and Stars

# INTRODUCTION

When you look up into the sky on a clear night, you can see what looks like thousands of little lights breaking through the darkness. What you may not know is that up there, farther than your eyes can see, are billions of objects in space. Besides the stars there are planets, moons, asteroids, meteorites, comets, galaxies and nebulas . . . just to name a few.

The study of outer space is called astronomy. Astronomers first learned the secrets of space by using telescopes. Looking into the sky they were able to see the stars and planets that are our neighbors. Soon stronger telescopes were built. Then astronauts were launched into space. They landed on the moon and brought back rocks that scientists studied. Probes were sent into space to travel to planets too far for people to reach. As these probes continue to travel farther from Earth, they send scientists pictures of other planets and stars, and we learn even more about our galaxy.

If you have a telescope or binoculars, you can use them to study space. Even if you don't have these tools, you can look with just your eyes and study the vast beauty of space. But you must never, NEVER, look directly at the sun. The beautiful, warm ball of fire can permanently damage and even blind your fragile eyes, even if you look for just a second.

This Take-Along Guide and its activities will help you find, identify, and learn about some of the things you see—and can't see—up in space. You can use the Scrapbook pages in the back of this book to draw what you see. Or you can draw things the way you imagine them to be. You can use the ruler on the back cover to help you track how the constellations and galaxies compare to each other in size.

Enjoy the sky full of planets, moons and stars!

# PLANETS & MOONS

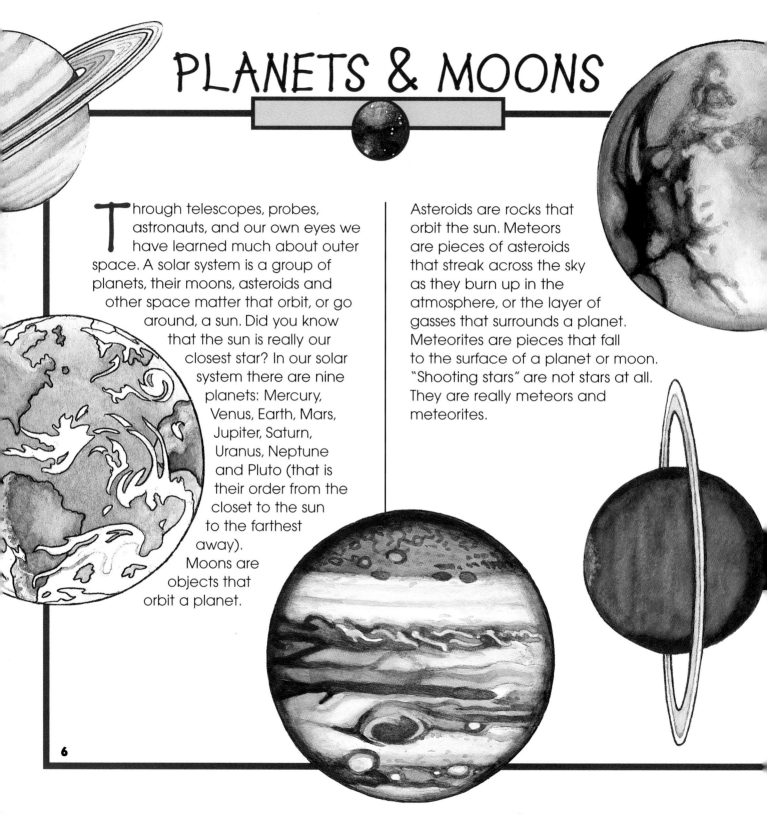

Through telescopes, probes, astronauts, and our own eyes we have learned much about outer space. A solar system is a group of planets, their moons, asteroids and other space matter that orbit, or go around, a sun. Did you know that the sun is really our closest star? In our solar system there are nine planets: Mercury, Venus, Earth, Mars, Jupiter, Saturn, Uranus, Neptune and Pluto (that is their order from the closet to the sun to the farthest away). Moons are objects that orbit a planet.

Asteroids are rocks that orbit the sun. Meteors are pieces of asteroids that streak across the sky as they burn up in the atmosphere, or the layer of gasses that surrounds a planet. Meteorites are pieces that fall to the surface of a planet or moon. "Shooting stars" are not stars at all. They are really meteors and meteorites.

The sky changes daily. As Earth orbits the sun, sunrise and sunset happen at different times. From one night to the next, the moon, stars and planets trace a path across the sky. You can follow the paths and track them throughout the year.

You can even track their movement in a single night. Notice the moon's place in the sky when you first see it at night, and then see where it is an hour later. And if you can stay up late, every hour after that.

When evening first comes, see how dark it is before the first star appears. Chances are the first "star" you see is actually a planet! Venus is sometimes called the "evening star" because you can see it shining before darkness falls. Soon you also may see Mercury or Mars. From this far away it is difficult to tell the difference between a planet and a star. A good thing to remember is that a star twinkles, like a flickering candle flame. A planet shines steadily, like a beam of light.

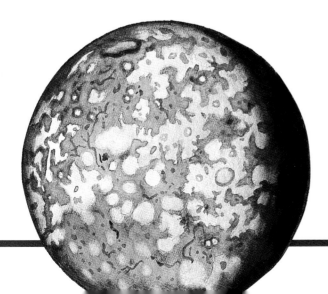

7

# MERCURY

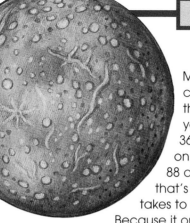

Mercury is the closest planet to the sun. While a year on Earth is 365 days, a year on Mercury is only 88 days, because that's how long it takes to orbit the sun. Because it orbits the sun faster than any other planet, it was named Mercury, after the speedy messenger god of Roman mythology.

The only planet smaller than Mercury is Pluto. Mercury is only a little larger than Earth's moon, and like the moon it is covered with craters. Many of the craters were made by asteroids crashing to the surface. Scientists think that an asteroid over 60 miles (96 kilometers) wide collided with Mercury and formed one of the largest craters in the solar system. It is over 800 miles (1,287 kilometers) wide and could hold the state of Texas. Mercury does not have a moon.

Mercury's core is made of solid iron. On top of the core there is probably a layer of liquid iron, and on top of that is the crust. Large amounts of molten lava were present in the core of Mercury during the time it was being struck by asteroids. The lava poured out of the craters and when it cooled, it formed large lava plains between them.

While it takes the Earth 24 hours to turn one full rotation, it takes Mercury almost 59 days to fully rotate. Mercury also has very little atmosphere. That means there is no blanket of air to keep the warmth close to the planet when it's not facing the sun. Because of how close it is to the sun and its little atmosphere, the temperature on Mercury can reach a scorching 840 degrees Fahrenheit (449 degrees Celsius) and drop to –290 degrees Fahrenheit (-179 degrees Celsius).

Mercury is not easy to view without a telescope, although it is possible. The best times to view Mercury are when it is farthest from the sun. During this period Mercury can be seen twice a year above the horizon just before sunset and sunrise.

### INTERESTING FACTS

The craters on Mercury are named for artists, writers, and composers such as Renoir, Brontë and Beethoven.

Take this book with you, and have fun!

# VENUS

Venus is the planet that passes the closest to Earth during its orbit. And because it is almost the same size as Earth, it is sometimes called Earth's twin. Venus is one of the brightest objects in the sky. It is always close to the sun and usually can be seen in the evening or early in the morning. It is so bright in the sky because it is completely covered with dense, yellow clouds that reflect the sunlight. Like Mercury, Venus does not have a moon.

Even through a telescope the surface of Venus is not visible. Below the clouds, which are made up of sulfuric acid, is an atmosphere of carbon dioxide gas. As sunlight filters through the layers of clouds, it heats up the planet and is partially trapped. This creates hot temperatures that sometimes rise to almost 900 degrees Fahrenheit (482 degrees Celsius), making Venus the hottest planet in the solar system.

The core of Venus is made up of iron and nickel. A thick, rocky mantle surrounds the core. On top of that is the surface of the planet, the crust. The crust of Venus is made of minerals that are found in sand and some rocks on Earth, called silicates.

Venus is named after the Roman goddess of love and beauty. Scientists named all of the land features on Venus after women, including Aphrodite, Cleopatra, Billie Holiday and Amelia Earhart. Only one mountain range was named after a man, Maxwell Montes. He was a scientist from Scotland whose research helped develop radar.

Scientists use radar to map the surface of Venus since it is not visible by telescope. There are many large craters on the surface as well as flat plains. Volcanoes created some domes and mountains. The highest point on Venus is seven miles (11.3 kilometers) high in the Maxwell Mountains. This is taller than Mount Everest, the highest place on Earth.

## INTERESTING FACTS

It takes Venus about 243 days to rotate once on its axis and 225 days to orbit the sun. That means that by the way we measure time, a day on Venus is longer than a year!

Find an open area with nothing blocking your view of the sky.

# EARTH

INTERESTING FACTS

Unlike all of the other planets, Earth is not named for a figure in Roman myth. It comes from the Old English word "eorthe."

Earth is the third planet from the sun, and while it has many things in common with the other planets in the solar system, it is also very unique. Like Mars and Venus, Earth has volcanoes. And like Mercury there are numerous craters. The Earth also has weather systems similar to the systems on Neptune and Jupiter.

But unlike any other planet in the solar system, evidence of life on Earth is visible from space. From space the Earth looks very blue. This is because of our oceans, which cover 70 percent of Earth's surface. While some planets have evidence of frozen water, only Earth contains both water in liquid form—our oceans, lakes and rivers—and frozen form—in glaciers, ice and snow. Planets closer to the Sun, such as Venus and Mercury, are too hot to have liquid water. It would evaporate.

Mars is too far away from the Sun to have anything but frozen water. Also, Earth has the only atmosphere in the solar system rich in oxygen, needed for the air that we breathe.

The atmosphere of the Earth is mostly a mix of oxygen, nitrogen, water and dust. The atmosphere is over 300 miles (480 kilometers) thick and fades into space. There are several different layers that make up the atmosphere.

The ozone is located in the layer of atmosphere called the stratosphere. It is a blanket of gases that protects the surface of Earth from harmful sun rays. The ozone layer has become thinner above the South Pole. Chemicals used in aerosol sprays may have caused the thinning. Small increases in Earth's temperature are believed to be caused by too many trees being cut down, especially in the rain forests. Also, carbon dioxide has been produced by burning great amounts of fuels such as coal and oil. Trees convert carbon dioxide in the atmosphere back into oxygen. With more carbon dioxide in the atmosphere, not as much heat caused by the sun's rays can escape from the planet and be released into space. Although we don't have the same atmosphere as Venus, this is the same reason why that planet is so hot.

Turn off outside lights and close the drapes to make it easier to see the stars.

The Earth rotates completely on its axis once every 24 hours. It takes the Earth 365 days to complete its orbit around the Sun.

The core, the mantle, and the outer shell are the three parts of Earth. The center of the planet is the core, which has inner and outer layers. The inner core is made up of solid iron and nickel. Around that is the hot, liquid outer core with a temperature of about 7,400 degrees Fahrenheit (4,100 degrees Celsius)! The mantle is on top of the liquid core. It makes up most of Earth's mass. Most of the mantle is solid, but some of it is believed to be molten rock. Above the mantle is the outer shell, made up of lithosphere and crust. The lithosphere is really plates that move against each other and change shape over time. The moving plates sometimes create volcanic eruptions and earthquakes. The crust is the top layer. It is the surface of Earth, like the skin on an apple.

## THE MOON

Our one moon is about 239,000 miles (385,000 kilometers) from Earth. The moon rotates completely on its axis about once every 27 days. It takes the same amount of time for the moon to complete its orbit around the Earth. Because of this, the same side of the moon faces the Earth at all times! Until astronauts were able to orbit the moon, no one had ever seen the other side. The side we can see is called the near side, and the side that cannot be seen from Earth is called the far side. You can see some details on the near side of the moon with binoculars. There are many craters on the surface of the moon caused by meteorites crashing into the surface. There is no life on the moon, and it has no liquid water.

Although the same side of the moon is always facing Earth, the moon does not always appear to be the same size or shape. This happens because the amount of sunlight shining onto the moon changes from day to day during the moon's orbit. When the sun shines on the far side of the moon, the near side is in its own shadow and cannot be seen from Earth. At this time it is called a "new moon." As the moon rotates around the Earth, you can see more of it. First you see a crescent, then a quarter. Eventually all of the near side is lit, and we call it a full moon. These are the moon's phases. It takes 29 days to go from new moon to full moon.

Earth is four times bigger than the moon. Some scientists believe that the moon was formed by fragments of Earth that flew into space when an object as big as a planet crashed into it billions of years ago. Eventually the fragments were pulled together and formed the mass of the moon.

Use binoculars or a telescope to help see the moon, stars, and planets.

# MARS

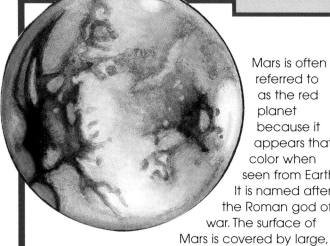

Mars is often referred to as the red planet because it appears that color when seen from Earth. It is named after the Roman god of war. The surface of Mars is covered by large, rocky deserts that are made up of rusty colored iron oxide. But unlike the hot deserts on Earth, the deserts on Mars are cold, and the iron oxide is frozen several miles deep. Mars has seasons like Earth, but with more extreme temperatures. The temperature on Mars is below freezing most of the time. In winter, the southern pole can be nearly -200 degrees Fahrenheit (-129 degrees Celsius). But in summer, the areas tilted closest to the sun can reach warm temperatures of 72 degrees Fahrenheit (22 degrees Celsius).

When Mars is closest to the sun and its temperature is at its hottest, and the wind speed is the fastest, the entire planet is sometimes covered in a dust storm.

Mars is about half the size of Earth, but it is not a very dense planet. For this reason it is only about a tenth of the mass of Earth. Like Earth, a day on Mars lasts about 24 hours. Mars is about one and a half times farther from the Sun than Earth. A year on Mars takes 687 Earth days.

Like Earth, Mars has clouds. Low areas sometimes have haze and fog, which are small amounts of water vapor in an atmosphere that is mostly carbon dioxide. Lots of ice can be found on Mars, especially on the South Pole. The size of the ice caps changes with the seasons, growing largest in the winter.

Take a flashlight along to help you find your way.

## MOONS

Mars has two moons named Phobos and Deimos. The names are Greek for "fear" and "panic." They have many craters. Scientists believe the moons are asteroids that were pulled into orbit by the planet's gravity.

The moons are made mostly of carbon and are very small. In diameter, the two moons are both too small to be seen from Earth without a large telescope. Like Earth's moon, the same side of Phobos always faces Mars.

Mars has many volcanic craters larger than any found on Earth. One huge volcano, Olympus Mons, is a mountain about 400 miles (644 kilometers) wide and over 16 miles (26 kilometers) high. That's three times higher than Earth's highest point, Mount Everest. White clouds often cover this volcano and can be seen with a telescope from Earth. A system of canyons, Valles Marineris, is about 2,800 miles (4,500 kilometers) long and looks like a dark line across the center of the planet.

You can sometimes see Mars without using a telescope. It looks like a bright orange star. Through a telescope you can see the north and south poles of Mars, and some of the bigger land features look like dark spots.

# JUPITER

Jupiter is the largest planet in our solar system. It is over twelve times wider than Earth and so massive that more than 1,000 Earths could fit inside of it. Jupiter weighs twice as much as all the other planets put together. Unlike Earth, Jupiter is a gas giant. Saturn, Neptune, and Uranus are also gas giants. This means that these large planets have several layers of dense gases below the clouds and a small rocky core. The gases that make up Jupiter are mostly liquid hydrogen and helium. Jupiter has faint rings around it made up of dust.

There are many violent storms in Jupiter's atmosphere. This is caused by Jupiter spinning very rapidly. It rotates once completely on its axis in less than ten hours.

Large amounts of heat trying to escape the layers of gas make the storms even more fierce. "The Great Red Spot" is on the southern part of Jupiter. The spot is actually a giant hurricane, over three times larger than Earth. The Great Red Spot rotates counterclockwise around the planet every six days.

The bands, called belts, on Jupiter are caused by rising and falling gas. Some of the belts are red, orange, blue, pink, yellow and brown, depending on what type of gas and other compounds, such as ammonia, make up the belt. The ring system around Jupiter was not discovered until 1975 when a probe called Voyager 1 sent back images.

Always wear shoes to protect your feet.

## MOONS

At this time, we know of 39 moons of Jupiter. Eleven of those were just discovered. The four largest moons were first studied in 1610 by the astronomer Galileo, and for him they are called the Galilean Moons.

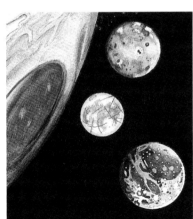

The largest of these is Ganymede, which is larger than the planet Mercury. Ganymede, and the second largest of Jupiter's moons, Callisto, are rocky with ice shells. There may be a salty ocean beneath the frozen crust of Callisto. The moon Europa, another Galilean moon, has a relatively smooth frozen surface. The ice surface has some cracks. Scientists think that heat from the center of the moon may be warming water underneath the ice crust and causing the cracks.

The fourth of the Galilean moons is Io. Io is the closest of the four Galilean moons to Jupiter and is the most volcanically active moon in our solar system. The volcanic activity is caused by the gravities of Jupiter, Europa, and Ganymede pulling it back and forth.

There are four smaller moons between Io and Jupiter. These moons are often struck by meteorites. The dust caused by these collisions makes Jupiter's rings.

# SATURN

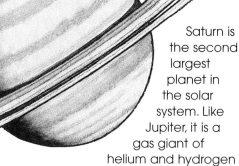

Saturn is the second largest planet in the solar system. Like Jupiter, it is a gas giant of helium and hydrogen with a small rocky core. It is nine times wider than Earth. Saturn is best known for its ring system. Even though Uranus, Jupiter, and Neptune have rings, Saturn's are by far the brightest. Three main rings can be seen with a telescope. There are actually seven different rings. Each ring is made up of many small ringlets of frozen chunks of rocks and ice. These chunks vary in size from as large as a house to smaller than pebbles.

Saturn rotates on its axis almost as fast as Jupiter, once about every 10 hours. It takes Saturn just over 29 Earth years to complete one orbit around the sun. As Saturn orbits around the sun it tilts, like Earth tilts as it orbits the sun. The rings are probably the remains of comets that became trapped in Saturn's gravity and then broke apart. Saturn's rings stretch out from the planet farther than any other planet's rings. The outer edge of the rings stretch out farther than the moon is from Earth.

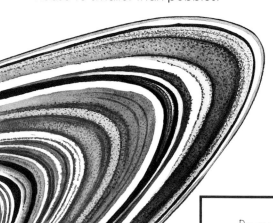

Be aware of changing weather.

Saturn is named after the father of Jupiter in Roman mythology. He was the god of agriculture and time.

## MOONS

Saturn has 18 moons that we know of. It may have even more. The Cassini space probe should arrive at Saturn in 2004. It will help us find out how many more there may be. Saturn's moons are made up of rock and ice, and some of them orbit within Saturn's rings. Two of the moons are only 32 miles (52 kilometers) apart. When they draw closest to each other every four years, they swap orbits—the inner moon takes the outer orbit and the outer moon takes the inner orbit. At one point these two moons may have been one but then split in half.

Titan is Saturn's largest moon. It is the only moon in the solar system that we know of with any atmosphere. Like Earth, the main gas on Titan is nitrogen. Unlike Earth, Titan is extremely cold, about -290 degrees Fahrenheit (-179 degrees Celsius). Because it is covered with orange smog, it is impossible to see the surface of Titan, even with a telescope.

Go inside as soon as you see lightning.

# URANUS

When you look at Uranus, the first thing you notice is that it looks like it is lying on its side. Its 11 rings circle the planet from top to bottom, instead of around the middle like Saturn. Some scientists think that Uranus was hit by a large object during its formation, tipping it on its side. Methane gas clouds give the planet its beautiful green-blue color. Uranus is the name of the sky god in Greek mythology.

Uranus is four times wider than Earth and orbits the sun once every 84 Earth years. It is 19 times farther away from the sun than Earth is. Although Uranus is the third largest planet in the solar system, it is so far away from Earth that it was not discovered until 1781 by a talented musician who had an interest in astronomy. Using a telescope he built for himself, William Herschel not only discovered Uranus, but also some of its moons and the moons of Saturn.

Explore safely. Go with a partner.

Because of the way it tilts, the seasons on Uranus last a very long time. There are 42 years of constant sunlight followed by 42 years of darkness at the north and south poles.

One day on Uranus lasts 17 hours and 14 minutes. It has winds of up to 375 miles (604 kilometers) per hour near its equator but does not have violent storms like those on Jupiter. Unlike Jupiter and Saturn, the gases that make up the mass of Uranus are mostly methane, ammonia, and water. Hydrogen is in the atmosphere, and temperatures are very cold in the upper clouds, about -330 degrees Fahrenheit (-201 degrees Celsius). The core of the planet is probably ice and rock. A layer of water and gas may exist just under the atmosphere.

## MOONS
Uranus has 20 moons that astronomers know of. The largest, Titania, is less than half the size of Earth's moon. The two moons farthest from the planet orbit in the opposite direction around the planet from all the other moons.

All of the moons are named after characters written by William Shakespeare and Alexander Pope. Besides Titania, some of the names are Juliet, Puck, Desdemona, and Ophelia.

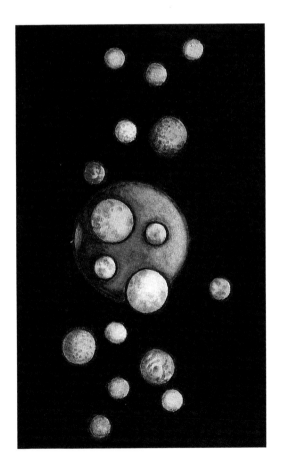

Tell an adult how long you will be gone.

# NEPTUNE

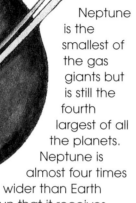

Neptune is the smallest of the gas giants but is still the fourth largest of all the planets. Neptune is almost four times wider than Earth and is so far from the sun that it receives less than a tenth of the sunlight of Earth. In many ways it is like Uranus, but Neptune looks more blue because the clouds that cover the planet have even more methane in them.

Neptune spins on its own axis about every 16 hours and takes almost 165 Earth years to orbit the sun. It is the windiest planet in the solar system, with winds of almost 1,300 miles (2,092 kilometers) per hour. In 1985 the Voyager 2 probe showed an image believed to be a large storm that was named the Great Dark Spot. But images that have been received since then show that it has disappeared.

Neptune has four rings that are made up of space dust and frozen rocks. Like the rings on Uranus, they are difficult to see. The rings were discovered when the planet passed in front of a star whose light made them appear to human eyes.

## INTERESTING FACTS

Because the color of the planet reminds us of the deep blue oceans, it is named after Neptune—the Roman god of the seas.

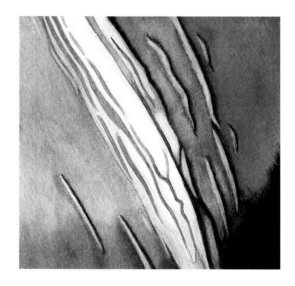

Watch where you step.

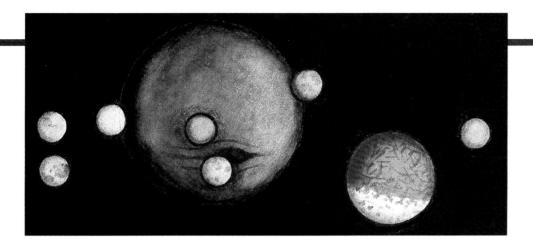

## MOONS

Neptune has eight moons that scientists know of. The four moons closest to the planet orbit in between the planet's rings. Because of this, some scientists think that the rings are made of dust from the surface of the moons.

The largest moon is called Triton, and it has the coldest surface of any moon or planet in the solar system. The temperature on Triton is sometimes colder than -390 degrees Fahrenheit (-234 degrees Celsius). It is covered by frozen methane and nitrogen. It is about two-thirds the size of Earth's moon.

Nitrogen gas erupts on the surface of Triton, then dust falls down to the surface of the moon. This is what makes the dark bands across the moon's surface.

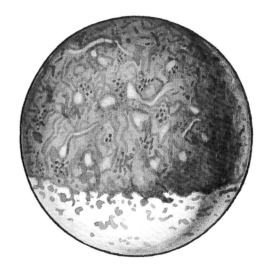

# PLUTO

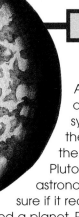

Pluto was discovered in 1930. Percival Lowell was the scientist who started the search for the planet.

At the far end of our solar system is Pluto, the smallest of the nine planets. Pluto is so small that astronomers are not sure if it really should be called a planet. Pluto is smaller than our moon and is only about one-fifth the size of Earth. Because a space probe has never reached Pluto, scientists guess what it is made of. The surface of Pluto is thought to be all rock and frozen methane. Under that there might be a layer of ice on top of a core of rock.

Pluto has an unusual shape to its orbit. It is far more oval shaped than any other planet's orbit. Because of this, Pluto is sometimes closer to the sun than Neptune. This happens for about 20 years of the almost 250 Earth years it takes Pluto to orbit once around the Sun. At its closest, Pluto is 2.8 billion miles (4.4 billion kilometers) from the sun. At its farthest, Pluto is 4.6 billion miles (7.4 billion kilometers) from the sun. When Pluto is close to the sun, some of the frozen material on the planet turns to gas and forms a thin atmosphere. Most of the time the planet is simply frozen and without atmosphere, with a cold surface temperature of -370 degrees Fahrenheit (-223 degrees Celsius). Pluto is named for the Greek god of the underworld.

## MOONS

Pluto has one moon named Charon. Both Charon and Pluto are made up of rock and ice and are covered with craters from meteorites crashing into them. Astronomers believe the moon may have been formed from ice knocked off Pluto by another object.

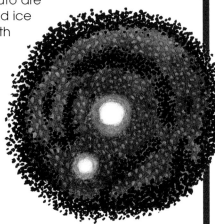

Plan a visit to a planetarium or science museum.

# Make a Planet Mobile

You can bring outer space into your room with this planet mobile.
Or you can make a mobile for one planet and its moons.

## WHAT YOU NEED
▼

- Several sheets of white paper
- Compass
- Scissors
- Crayons, markers, or watercolor paints
- Nine pieces of string, cut to different lengths
- Glue
- 2 wire clothes hangers
- 2 twist-ties or small pieces of wire
- Newspaper

## WHAT TO DO
▼

1 Cover the top of the table with newspaper.

2 Put one hanger through the other to make an X. Wrap one twist-tie around and through the necks of the hangers to hold them together. Twist the other tie around the middle of the bottom of the hangers where they cross one another. This is the base of your mobile.

3 Draw two circles for each planet. You can use the compass to help you draw perfect circles. You can make all the planets the same size, or you can make some bigger and some smaller. Here is the order of the planets from biggest to smallest:

| | | |
|---|---|---|
| #1 Jupiter | #4 Neptune | #7 Mars |
| #2 Saturn | #5 Earth | #8 Mercury |
| #3 Uranus | #6 Venus | #9 Pluto |

4 Color one circle of each of the pairs to look like a different planet. Be sure to draw craters and volcanoes if the planet has them. Color the second circle of each pair to look exactly like the first.

5 Cut out the circles. Keep the pairs together.

6 Glue the end of a piece of string between the two matching circles of one planet. Make sure the colored sides are both facing out. Do this for all the planets.

7 Hang all the planets on the mobile.

8 Have a grown-up help you hang your mobile.

# STARS

S tars are the twinkling points of light that we see in the night sky. Each point of light is actually a huge ball of gas that generates heat and light just like our sun. The reason the stars look so tiny compared to the sun is because they are much farther away from Earth. From the other side of the galaxy our sun looks like a tiny point of light, too.

A constellation is an area of space that has a boundary around a group of stars. Many constellations have stars that look like they are arranged in a pattern. Centuries ago, people named the patterns after gods and characters in their mythology, or legends. The stories helped them remember the patterns and their locations in the sky. By finding them at night and following their paths across the sky, they were able to travel the land and navigate the seas without getting lost.

Twelve constellations belong to a group called the zodiac. The zodiac constellations are lined up in a band. As Earth orbits the sun, the sun "passes through" each of these constellations at different times of the year. Ages ago, people named these constellations and linked them to the dates that the sun was in front of them. When someone was born, they were said to have the "sign" of the zodiac constellation for their birth date. Over the centuries, Earth's orbit has changed. And although the dates for each sign are the same as they were

then, the sun is no longer in the zodiac constellations at the same time.

One of the most beautiful sights in dark space is a nebula. Nebulas are clouds of dust and gas that are the birthplace and graveyard of stars. Some nebulas have brilliant colors, lit up by the stars within. Some do not shine at all.

We are part of the Milky Way galaxy. A galaxy is a group of stars that is linked together by gravity. Billions of stars can be in the same galaxy.

# SUN

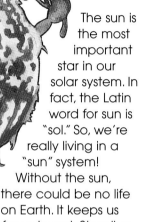

The sun is the most important star in our solar system. In fact, the Latin word for sun is "sol." So, we're really living in a "sun" system! Without the sun, there could be no life on Earth. It keeps us warm and grows food for us to eat. Stars live about 10 billion years, and scientists believe the sun has been alive for about half that time already. The sun is a huge ball of gas. It is over a hundred times bigger than Earth. Its mass is about 750 times more than all of the planets in our solar system put together.

The sun has different layers. Like the planets, the sun has a core. The temperature at the core is 59 million degrees Fahrenheit (nearly 33 million degrees Celsius)! All of the sun's energy is generated in the core.

Sometimes there are dark blotches on the sun. These are called sunspots. They are caused by magnetic forces inside the sun that keep the gases from rising to the surface. Some are as small as 620 miles (998 kilometers) across while some are as big as 62,000 miles (99,780 kilometers) across! The spots disappear over time.

Explosions above sunspots can happen when the energy is released. They are called solar flares. The burst of sun particles and radiation has an effect on us. They can stop radio waves and endanger astronauts when they travel in space. Flares can last several hours.

As the moon orbits around Earth, it sometimes travels directly in front of the sun, blocking it from view from different places on the planet. This is called a solar eclipse. Sometimes only a part of the sun is blocked and sometimes it is totally blocked. This is a strange sight, especially when it happens during the daytime. When a total solar eclipse happens, it can seem like night. You can even see some stars!

NEVER look directly into the sun.

# ANDROMEDA

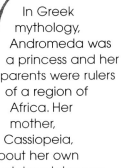

INTERESTING FACTS

In a dark sky, the Andromeda Galaxy is the farthest thing from Earth that can be seen with the naked eye.

In Greek mythology, Andromeda was a princess and her parents were rulers of a region of Africa. Her mother, Cassiopeia, bragged about her own beauty. She claimed she was so beautiful that she was even more beautiful than the sea nymphs. Outraged at this claim, the ruler of the sea, Poseidon, sent a giant sea monster, Cetus, to destroy them. Andromeda's parents were told they would be spared if they gave up their daughter. They chained Andromeda to a rock along the sea.

Perseus was riding above in the sky on his horse, Pegasus, and saw Andromeda below. He swooped down on Pegasus' back and rescued Andromeda by turning the giant monster to stone.

Andromeda does not contain very bright stars. The constellation is shaped as though Andromeda is leaning to one side. The constellation contains the Andromeda Galaxy, which is the closest large galaxy to our own. The Andromeda Galaxy is very similar to our Milky Way. It is a spiral galaxy and contains over 200 billion stars. Andromeda also contains a beautiful double star. One of the stars is golden yellow, and the other is a greenish blue. Both can be seen from Earth with binoculars.

The best time to look for Andromeda is in October and November.

Be patient and use your imagination when finding constellations.

# CANIS MAJOR

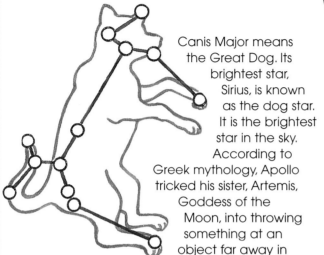

Canis Major means the Great Dog. Its brightest star, Sirius, is known as the dog star. It is the brightest star in the sky. According to Greek mythology, Apollo tricked his sister, Artemis, Goddess of the Moon, into throwing something at an object far away in the sea. He did this because he felt that Artmeis was not doing her work of lighting the sky because she was too busy thinking of Orion. The object turned out to be Orion swimming and, as a result of being hit in the head, he died. Artemis, feeling sad about what she had done, put Orion in the sky with his two dogs, Canis Major and Canis Minor.

Canis Major can be found by following the three stars that make up Orion's belt to the southeast.

Sirius has been blamed for the hot days at the end of summer. This is because in the late summer, the bright Sirius rises at the same time as the sun. There is no proof that this makes the temperature on Earth hotter, but it does explain why people often call August "the dog days of summer." Sirius is less than nine light years from Earth and is 40 times brighter than the sun.

## INTERESTING FACTS

A small star orbits Sirius, the dog star, every 50 years. It is called the Pup!

Get permission before going onto someone's land.

# CASSIOPEIA

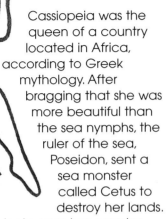

Cassiopeia was the queen of a country located in Africa, according to Greek mythology. After bragging that she was more beautiful than the sea nymphs, the ruler of the sea, Poseidon, sent a sea monster called Cetus to destroy her lands. In order to save her country, Cassiopeia and her husband decided to sacrifice their daughter, Andromeda. Their daughter was rescued by a man flying overhead on Pegasus. It was believed because of her boastful ways, Cassiopeia was chained to her throne and put in the sky for punishment.

In 1937 it was the brightest star in the "W" and now it is only the third brightest of those stars. Another star in this constellation pulsates in a pattern that takes a little under a year to complete, with its brightness changing during the cycle.

Cassiopeia is located north of her daughter, Andromeda, and west of her husband, Cepheus. She is usually shown sitting vainly on her throne.

## INTERESTING FACTS

One of the stars in this constellation spins so fast that it throws off rings of gas at its center, causing its brightness to constantly change.

The brightest stars form what appears to be a tilting "W" or "M" depending on the time of year. This well-known shape makes Cassiopeia an easy constellation to find in the sky. The third star in this shape has lost some of its brightness over the years.

Walk carefully so you do not injure any plants.

# HERCULES

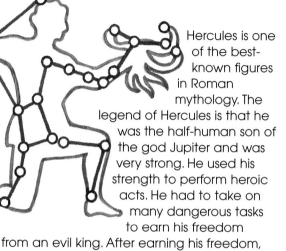

Hercules is one of the best-known figures in Roman mythology. The legend of Hercules is that he was the half-human son of the god Jupiter and was very strong. He used his strength to perform heroic acts. He had to take on many dangerous tasks to earn his freedom from an evil king. After earning his freedom, he continued to do many brave deeds. When he died, his father, Jupiter, placed him in the sky forever.

The constellation is best seen in the summer, although none of its stars are very bright. It is thought to be one the oldest constellations.

For people who live in North America, four stars forming a shape called a keystone are easy to find. This shape makes up the body of Hercules. The constellation's legs and arms are all bent, and it takes some imagination to see Hercules, who is running and holding something high above his head.

Hercules contains the brightest globular cluster in the northern hemisphere. A globular cluster is a round group of stars that may contain thousands and sometimes millions of stars. They are located on the far edges of the Milky Way.

INTERESTING FACTS

Many of the beasts that Hercules defeated are also constellations, including Hydra and Taurus.

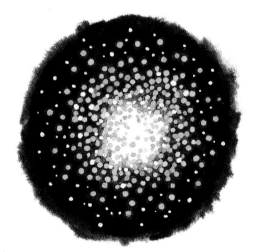

30

Pay attention to everything around you.

# LYRA

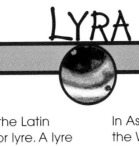

Lyra is the Latin word for lyre. A lyre is a small harp often played while singing or reading poetry in Greece. The legend behind the constellation Lyra is that it is the lyre that Apollo, the Greek god of poetry and music, gave to his son, Orpheus. When his wife died and was taken to the underworld, he was able to get her back by playing his lyre beautifully for Hades. Orpheus was told he could not look at his wife until he had completely left the underworld. In his excitement, he looked at her just before they left, and she was swept back to Hades. Following his death, Orpheus was reunited with his wife, and Zeus placed his lyre in the sky.

Lyra is a small constellation but it is easy to identify its shape. Lyra contains the brilliant star Vega. Vega sits on top of Lyra and is the fifth brightest star in the sky. This bright star has its own legend.

In Asia, Vega is called the Weaving-Princess Star. The legend is that the princess fell in love with a shepherd, the star Altair. They were punished by her father when they both ignored their responsibilities and were put on opposite sides of the galaxy. These two stars only appear close together once a year in the middle of the summer and then drift far apart to opposite sides of the sky.

The best months to see Lyra are July through August.

With a telescope you can see the Ring Nebula in the constellation. At first it may look like a star that's out of focus, but If you look closer you can see the beautiful colors and its shape.

## INTERESTING FACTS

Arab astronomers thought this constellation looked like an eagle. Vega is Arabic for "soaring eagle."

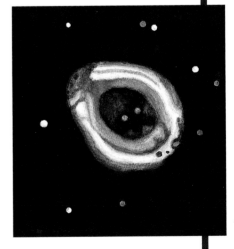

# ORION

Orion may look like the figure it was named for more than any other constellation. It is easy to recognize in the night sky. In Greek mythology he is a giant and a hunter. The constellation has him with a club in one hand and the skin of a lion in the other. The three bright stars that make up his belt and the fourth that makes up his dagger can be seen with the naked eye in most of the world from December to April.

There are many interesting things in the Orion constellation. His left foot is a star known as Rigel. This star is about 1,400 light years away and is believed to be 50,000 times brighter than the sun. The Orion Nebula, also called the Great Nebula, can be seen with the naked eye in a dark sky, or even better with a telescope.

This Nebula has four bright stars that are young in age. Astronomers believe that this is a star nursery and that new stars are actually born in this nebula.

The Horsehead Nebula is also found in Orion. The shape is of a dark horse's head against a beautiful background of red.

**32**

Use the Scrapbook to draw what you see.

# PEGASUS

Pegasus was a great flying horse in mythology. The legend is that after the son of Zeus, Perseus, killed the hideous Gorgon Medusa, Pegasus sprang from the drops of her blood that mixed with sea foam. The Gorgon Medusa was so ugly that when men looked at her they turned to stone. While returning from this battle, Perseus saw Andromeda tied to a rock and about to be attacked by a sea monster. Riding Pegasus into the danger, they saved Andromeda.

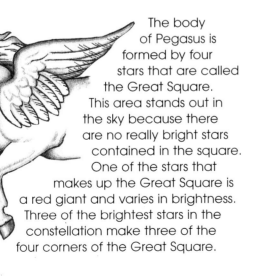

The body of Pegasus is formed by four stars that are called the Great Square. This area stands out in the sky because there are no really bright stars contained in the square. One of the stars that makes up the Great Square is a red giant and varies in brightness. Three of the brightest stars in the constellation make three of the four corners of the Great Square.

The nose of Pegasus is the star Enif, which is the Arabic word for nose. The front legs of Pegasus are easy to locate in the night sky. The constellation does not have rear legs.

The best time to see Pegasus is from July to September.

INTERESTING FACTS

Some astronomers believe that when ancient cultures first identified the constellation as a horse, stars may have been visible that looked like rear legs.

Wear reflective tape and light colors when out at night.

# SAGITTARIUS

Sagittarius is a zodiac constellation. If your birthday is between November 22 and December 21, this is your sign. Sagittarius is usually pictured as an archer with his bow and arrow pointed at Scorpius. The lower half of Sagittarius is that of a horse, making him half man and half horse, called a centaur. The constellation is said to honor Crotus, the inventor of archery in Greek mythology and the son of the Greek god Pan.

When you see Sagittarius you are looking toward the center of the Milky Way and the fields of stars are very thick in this direction.

Sagittarius contains a well-known group of eight stars referred to as the Teapot. These stars form a teapot with a long spout and lid

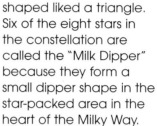

shaped liked a triangle. Six of the eight stars in the constellation are called the "Milk Dipper" because they form a small dipper shape in the star-packed area in the heart of the Milky Way.

The brightest star in the constellation is named Rukbat. Rukbat is Arabic for knee, and it is found in the knee of the front right leg of the centaur. Another star below Rukbat is named Arkab, the Arabic word for Achilles tendon.

The best time to look for Sagittarius is in July and August.

Sagittarius contains over a dozen of the most popular items to search for in the sky, including the Lagoon Nebula, the Trifid Nebula, and the Omega Nebula. Nebulas are huge clouds of gas and dust.

Take an extra long look at the night sky when away from bright city lights.

# SCORPIUS

The constellation Scorpius is named after the tiny scorpion that killed Orion in Greek mythology. Scorpius and the constellation Orion are found on opposite sides of the sky, which means that Orion sets as Scorpius rises. Scorpius is one of the twelve constellations that make up the zodiac. If your birthday is between October 23 and November 21 your zodiac sign is Scorpio.

The hooked tail of Scorpius is made up of nine bright stars that really help you locate the constellation. Originally Scorpius included stars that made up large claws. The stars that made up the claws are now part of the Libra constellation.

Scorpius is found along the Milky Way and so it has many stars within the constellation. There are several star clusters that can be seen with binoculars. One star cluster is located just above the top of the hooked tail. It is called M7 and is 780 light years away from Earth.

These stars are bright enough that they can be seen against the brightness of the Milky Way.

Scorpius contains a supergiant called Antares. This is the brightest star of Scorpius. It has a reddish color like the planet Mars. Its name translated means "anti," or against, and "Ares," or Mars. So its name means "rival of Mars."

The best time to see Scorpius is June and July.

### INTERESTING FACTS

In Scorpius, the red star Antares is located in the same place that the heart of a scorpion would really be found.

Do not point a flashlight into the eyes of a person or animal.

# TAURUS

Taurus is another zodiac constellation. If your birthday is between April 20 and May 20, your sign is Taurus. Thousands of years ago the appearance of Taurus in the sky signaled the beginning of spring to ancient civilizations. For this reason it is not surprising that Taurus means bull, an animal that symbolizes strength. In Greek mythology the powerful Zeus turned himself into a bull so he could enter the country of Crete and swim away with a princess on his back.

The constellation of Taurus only shows the front half of the bull, with two bright stars clearly showing the tips of the horns. There are two major star clusters in Taurus; one of them, Hyades, makes up the face of the bull.

The other star cluster is called Pleiades. They were the seven daughters of Atlas and Pleione. For this reason this star cluster is often referred to as the "Seven Sisters." The Seven Sisters are located in the upper shoulder of Taurus. The brightest star, Aldebaran, is a red giant located on the face of the bull. It looks like the bull's bloodshot eye.

The best time to see Taurus is in December and January.

### INTERESTING FACTS

The Seven Sisters cluster is made up of hundreds of stars. But only six, not seven, can be seen from Earth with the naked eye.

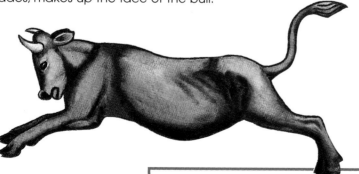

Take this book and a pencil when you go exploring.

# URSA MAJOR

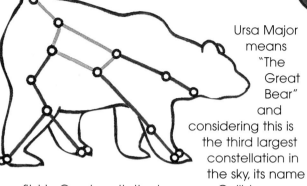

In England the Big Dipper is often called the Plough. The cup of the Big Dipper is seen as a plough blade, and the handle of the Big Dipper is a pair of horses pulling the blade.

Ursa Major means "The Great Bear" and considering this is the third largest constellation in the sky, its name fits! In Greek myth the bear was Callisto, a hunting partner of Artemis turned into a bear by the jealous wife of Zeus.

Ursa Major is best known for containing the bright stars that form the Big Dipper. The handle of the Big Dipper forms the tail of the Great Bear. If you follow a line from the star that is the bottom right corner of the Big Dipper through the star that is the top right corner, you will find Polaris, the North Star. Polaris is part of the Little Dipper.

Ursa Major is much larger than just the Big Dipper. Many stars that are not part of the Big Dipper form the outline of the bear. Many of the stars in Ursa Major have Arabic names, including stars whose names mean " bear," "flank," "thigh" and "root of tail."

Ursa Major is most visible in February to May.

Do not shout or yell when outside at night so neighbors are not disturbed.

# URSA MINOR

Ursa Minor means "The Little Bear." Greek legend says that when Zeus' wife Hera became jealous of Callisto and forced her into the sky as Ursa Major, Hera also cast Callisto's son Arcas with her. He became Ursa Minor. Both bears are said to rotate around the north star so they never touch land or sea again.

Ursa Minor is also called the Little Dipper. You have to use your imagination to find the rest of the shape of the little bear. Unlike Ursa Major, there are no stars that clearly mark the body of this bear.

Polaris, the North Star, is the tip of the bear's tail and the end of the handle of the Little Dipper. The North Star has been an important star for hundreds of years because it is located in almost the exact location of the sky's north pole. Since it is fairly bright and never sets in the sky, sailors and explorers learned to rely on it. They realized that if they located the North Star they knew which way was north and how to find their way.

The North Star is not the brightest star in the sky. It is really only the 49th brightest star.

The best time to see Ursa Minor is from May through June.

## INTERESTING FACTS

The North Star, located in the tip of the tail of Ursa Minor, is fully visible to anyone in the northern hemisphere at all times.

Watch the news for information on eclipses, meteor showers, and passing comets.

# VIRGO

Virgo is the second largest of all the constellations.

Virgo is the only constellation of the zodiac of a female. Many cultures said she was a goddess of fertility, justice, or agriculture. When Virgo is portrayed as a goddess of justice, she is seen holding the scales of Libra, which is the constellation next to her. Virgo is the largest of the twelve constellations that make up the zodiac. If your birthday is between August 23 and September 22, this is your sign.

The Virgo Cluster is in the constellation. It is the closest large cluster of galaxies to Earth. This cluster may contain more than 2,000 galaxies over 50 million light years away from Earth.

Virgo is best seen from April to June.

### INTERESTING FACTS

Another galaxy seen in Virgo is called the Sombrero Galaxy. It got its name because from Earth it looks like a large flat hat.

Virgo's brightest star, Spica, is in her left hand. Spica is Latin for "ear of wheat." Virgo is often shown holding a shaft of wheat. This star is one of the twenty brightest stars in the sky.

Use the ruler on the back of this book to measure the difference in the size of constellations.

# Find Your Own Constellation

Your can find and name your own constellation and keep track of its path across the sky.

## WHAT YOU NEED

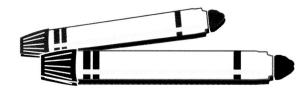

- This book, turned to a blank Scrapbook page, or a notebook
- Flashlight
- Crayons or markers in red, blue and black
- Binoculars (if you want)
- A dark, starry night with no clouds in the sky

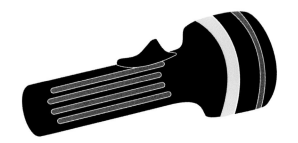

## WHAT TO DO

**1** Look at the stars until your eyes are used to the dark. Find a constellation or two that you recognize. You can use binoculars if you'd like. Look at stars that are not part of the constellations you know. See if a pattern jumps out at you and makes you think of an animal, a person, or an object.

**2** Keeping track of the location of your new constellation, find a constellation close by that already exists, like the Big Dipper or Orion.

**3** Draw the stars of the old constellation with the black marker. Then draw the stars for your new constellation on the page using the red marker (you can connect the stars for both if you want to make an outline). Draw it on the paper exactly where it is in the sky from the old constellation.

**4** Use the blue marker to draw other stars and objects in space that lie between the constellations and around it. They will help you find your new constellation again later.

**5** Give your new constellation a name.

**6** Skywatch again in a couple of days. Can you still find the constellation you named? Has it moved in the sky?

## OTHER IDEAS:

- Write a story about the figure in your constellation. Tell what happened to it during its life and how it came to be part of the stars. Tell how it's related to other figures in the constellations.
- Draw a picture of what the figure in your constellation really looks like. If it is an animal, draw the body and fur. If it is a person, draw the face and clothes. Maybe it's an object like a car or roller coaster!
- Watch your constellation for a year. Write down what months are the best times to see it.

# SCRAPBOOK

Planets, Moons and Stars

# Find All Kinds of Stuff...

# Take-Along Guides

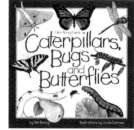

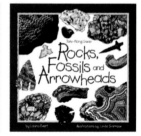

## Titles available in the Take-Along Guide series:

Berries, Nuts and Seeds
ISBN 1-55971-573-1

Birds, Nests and Eggs
ISBN 1-55971-624-X

Caterpillars, Bugs
and Butterflies
ISBN 1-55971-674-6

Frogs, Toads and Turtles
ISBN 1-55971-593-6

Planets, Moons and Stars
ISBN 1-55971-842-0

Rabbits, Squirrels
and Chipmunks
ISBN 1-55971-579-0

Rocks, Fossils
and Arrowheads
ISBN 1-55971-786-6

Seashells, Crabs
and Sea Stars
ISBN 1-55971-675-4

Snakes, Salamanders
and Lizards
ISBN 1-55971-627-4

Tracks, Scats and Signs
ISBN 1-55971-599-5

Trees, Leaves and Bark
ISBN 1-55971-628-2

Wildflowers, Blooms
and Blossoms
ISBN 1-55971-642-8

## See your nearest bookseller, or order by phone 1-800-328-3895

NORTHWORD PRESS
Chanhassen, Minnesota